Recognizing Bias

Aidan M. Ryan

Cavendish
Square
New York

Published in 2019 by Cavendish Square Publishing, LLC
243 5th Avenue, Suite 136, New York, NY 10016

Library of Congress Cataloging-in-Publication Data

Names: Ryan, Aidan M.
Title: Recognizing bias / Aidan M. Ryan.
Description: New York : Cavendish Square, 2019. | Series:
News literacy | Includes glossary and index.
Identifiers: ISBN 9781502641434 (pbk.) | ISBN 9781502641441
(library bound) | ISBN 9781502641458 (ebook)
Subjects: LCSH: Social media--Psychological aspects--Juvenile
literature. | Prejudices--Juvenile literature. | Belief and doubt--
Juvenile literature. | Disinformation--Juvenile literature.
Classification: LCC HM742.R94 2019 | DDC 302.23'1--dc23

Editorial Director: David McNamara
Editor: Caitlyn Miller
Copy Editor: Lisa Goldstein
Associate Art Director: Alan Sliwinski
Designer: Joe Parenteau
Production Coordinator: Karol Szymczuk
Photo Research: J8 Media

CONTENTS

Much of the information we take in each day does not come from our firsthand experiences. Instead, it comes from TV, newspapers, books, online articles, social media posts, and more.

Approaching and Understanding Bias

Today, most of the information people receive is about faraway places and events that can't be verified firsthand. Students take in information about ancient Roman games and present-day sports teams. We read, see, or hear news about battles in Sudan, elections in Afghanistan, protests in Spain, and celebrations in Australia. This information comes from a flood of different media. Media sources include newspapers, textbooks, Snapchat stories, talk radio shows, TV programs, podcasts, YouTube videos and ads, articles in a Facebook news feed, emails, and even memes.

Every piece of news, from all over the world, is a version of reality. Here, global newspapers report on the September 11 terrorist attacks.

When processing this constant flood of information, it's important to remember that every bit from every source comes from another human being. All humans understand reality differently. All humans, at least part of the time, *want* reality to be different than it really is. And most humans want to convince other humans that their version of reality is the right one.

The Basics of Bias: What It Is and Where It Comes From

There is often a difference between the information that people can access and the information people accept and share with others. This difference is bias.

Basically, a bias is a form of preference. This could be a preference for one statement, one story, one person or group, or one version of reality over others. This preference is rooted in feelings rather than facts. Through bias, people's feelings shape the facts that they accept. It affects the way people think, form opinions, and make decisions.

Bias is a characteristic all people have—but it's one that few want to admit having. A bias can be a tendency to make unfair judgments about people or groups—the way sports fans often make unfair judgments about rival teams, players, or other fans. A bias can also be a tendency to approach situations and choices in a certain manner, often in a way that is unfair or unreasonable.

You can think of bias as a bad habit that happens in your mind. Like other bad habits, biases can be very hard to recognize and control. Also like other habits, biases can be relatively harmless. A graduate of the University of Kentucky might have a bias for all things related to the Wildcats. Her closet might be full of clothes in Kentucky Blue, and she might fiercely argue with anyone who says another school's teams are better. This isn't hurting anyone. Yet it's important to understand that even harmless biases can create new, more dangerous ones.

Imagine that the same woman becomes a manager at a company, and her preference for Kentucky makes her biased in favor of other people who went to the school. Even though the root bias (loving a sports team) seems harmless, it is now having an effect on the lives of dozens of people. She's begun to treat job applicants unfairly,

E. B. WHITE ON SLANT

"I have yet to see a piece of writing, political or non-political, that does not have a slant. All writing slants the way a writer leans, and no man is born perpendicular."

—E. B. White

E. B. White was the author of the children's books *Stuart Little* and *Charlotte's Web*. He was also a writer for *New Yorker* magazine, and he cowrote a short book on how to write well, called *The Elements of Style*. In the quote above, he explains that everyone has a bias, or a slant. He says no one is born perpendicular, or standing at a ninety-degree angle with the earth, and these biases will come out in what we write and say.

E. B. White lived from 1899 to 1985. He wrote many books, including three books for children.

White believed that people cannot escape their biases. However, he tried, in everything he said and wrote, to think reasonably, to judge fairly, and to tell the truth.

and perhaps she's not hiring the best employees for the company. The most dangerous part is that she might not be aware of the bias at all. That means she's unlikely ever to correct it, and the problems her bias is causing will only spread and get worse.

Bias and News Media

It's hard to recognize and correct our own biases. That's not all we have to worry about, either. We also have to spot (and correct) other people's biases. Our friends have biases. Facebook posts and tweets have biases. Additionally, we find biases coming from people and

The rise of the internet has given biased news media more avenues for entering our lives.

sources that we learn to trust, like parents, teachers, and religious figures.

Then there are biases in newspapers, TV stories, talk radio programs, web articles, and books. (Even dictionaries have biases.) Because these sources are media, this type of bias is called media bias. The plural word "media," like the singular "medium," comes directly from Latin, and means "middle." A medium is like a filter. Information passes through the filter of different media sources: magazines, websites, Twitter accounts, books, documentaries, and more. Over time, people started to use the term "the media" to refer not only to the sources—books and newspapers, back then—but also to the people behind them. Eventually, most people understood "the media" to mean all of the sources of news and all of the journalists, filmmakers, producers, researchers, and others who make news. "Media bias," then, came to mean a widespread "unfairness" across all sources of news.

Media bias can appear in surprising places. The weather may not seem like a source of media bias, but plenty of TV reporters have revealed their biases by exaggerating reports of extreme weather—and getting caught. The most famous may be Michelle Kosinski, who, as a journalist for NBC, reported on heavy rains in Wayne, New Jersey, *while paddling a canoe*. This would have made for a very impressive display of the amount and power of the rain ... but unfortunately for Kosinski, two men walked across the shot, in front of her boat, sloshing through ankle-deep water.

Journalist Lucy Yang must not have been watching the news that day. Five years later, reporting for a local ABC station in New Jersey, she arranged a shot of nine people floating in inflatable boats at an intersection, claiming the boats were "the only way" they could cross the street. Media history repeated itself when another man walked across the shot—again, in water only up to his ankles.

In both cases, these TV reporters weren't intentionally trying to make any person or group look good or bad. However, their mild bias—a preference—for dramatic stories about damage, danger, and hardship, led them into irresponsible reporting. News that exaggerates like this can make ordinary people panic. It can also (unfairly) make public servants and elected officials, like mayors and police chiefs and hospital workers, look unprepared and ineffective.

Of course, journalists aren't the only ones exaggerating the weather because of biases. Politicians do it all the time, trying to influence people toward their way of thinking about issues like climate change, land conservation, natural resources, natural disasters, pollution, and government spending.

Beyond the weather, think about all the sources of biased information and opinions that people encounter in just one day. Bias surrounds us everywhere. And, like germs in the air during a never-ending flu season, bias is contagious. People can pick up biases from friends, teachers, parents—anyone. But even if bias can't be cured or completely eliminated, it is possible to identify it, treat it, and stop it from spreading.

We call TV and magazines "media" because information passes through them. Like light through water or glass, news media change the angle of what passes through.

Navigating the Misinformation Age

People often say that biased statements, stories, or decisions are "slanted." The English word "bias" actually comes from the French word *biais*, which means an angle or a slanting line. The slant in this sense is like the slant that appears to happen when objects are lowered into clear water. Bias works like water, when it changes the angle of something that passes through it. Instead of light, though, bias puts a slant into information. Any information that passes through someone's bias gets bent at a new angle too.

Individuals are biased because certain facts, opinions, and stories make us each feel safe, happy, proud, or correct. These are good feelings, and our brains

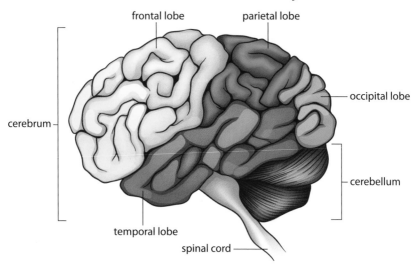

Human Brain Anatomy

frontal lobe

parietal lobe

occipital lobe

cerebrum

cerebellum

temporal lobe

spinal cord

The brain is a complex machine that works not only to process information for decision-making but also to reward us with positive feelings.

are machines that feed us those good feelings. Each day, the brain processes an incredible amount of data, including images, sounds, conversations, daydreams, and other people's body language. Brains work to filter out the data that would make us feel negative emotions and hold on to the data that makes us feel positive emotions. If a person receives a compliment, his or her brain holds on to the compliment. If a person is criticized, his or her brain may not be able to block it out completely, but it is likely to invent excuses to deflect the insult or criticism.

A Brief History of Trust and Distrust in the Media

All humans have these tendencies to bend, warp, exclude, or even invent information. However, we trust certain people to control their biases more than others. We do not often think about this trust. We trust because we have no other option. From birth, babies trust their parents to make rational decisions to protect them. Students trust teachers to explain the way things work, like chemical reactions and grammar. Citizens trust the government and its employees to do all sorts of things—from putting out fires to making sure that foods and medicines are safe.

Ideally, most people would also trust the news media to find the truth, to tell the truth, and to make sure other groups—like the government, teachers, and powerful businesses—tell the truth too. However, the amount of trust that average people have in the media has changed quite a lot over time. A decline in trust often follows changes in the ways people get the news.

John Peter Zenger and Freedom of the Press

In America, there is a very old belief in the power of the media to check the power of the government. This idea took firm root in 1733, when "America" was still a collection of British colonies. A German immigrant named John Peter Zenger had come with his family to New York City and had started business as a newspaper publisher. He happened to publish something that was critical of New York's colonial governor, William Cosby. In 1733, Cosby had Zenger arrested and charged him with libel, or the printing of a false statement that harms someone's reputation. Until this point, governments could use libel charges to harass, run out of business, or imprison

The John Peter Zenger trial influenced the American understanding of what a free press can (and should) do to check the powers of the government.

anyone critical of them. But Zenger's lawyers argued that what Zenger had printed was true and therefore could not be libel. The jury declared Zenger innocent.

This idea was "revolutionary." Following the American Revolution, the Founding Fathers set it down in the Bill of Rights as the First Amendment, which protects freedom of speech and of the press (today, known as the media). Since then, American citizens have relied on news media to tell the truth when other groups would not. In the 1970s, brave reporters, editors, and publishers at different papers wrote stories that showed the Kennedy, Johnson, and Nixon presidential administrations had been lying to the American people about the Vietnam War and other issues.

In 2013, the British publication the *Guardian* reported on leaked documents that revealed the American government had been spying on citizens using advanced computer technologies. And in October 2017, *New York Times* reporters Jodi Kantor and Megan Twohey published reporting that exposed the Hollywood producer Harvey

Journalists Jodi Kantor (*left*) and Megan Twohey (*right*) were awarded a Pulitzer Prize in 2018 for their work.

EDWARD R. MURROW AND THE "WORLD IN WHICH WE LIVE"

Few people deserve more credit for giving Americans reason to trust in the media than Edward R. Murrow. Born in 1908, Murrow started working for CBS Radio at a time when most breaking news reports came from newspapers—once in the morning and once in the evening. Radio journalists did not report live—certainly not the way journalists today can immediately reach their audiences through Twitter, Snapchat, and other platforms. Instead, they read pre-written accounts of what was happening around the world.

In 1937, Murrow moved abroad to lead CBS' European operations. When Adolf Hitler's Germany captured Austria that year, Murrow's team delivered some of the first reports on the events. He soon became known for pioneering live coverage during World War II, including vivid reports from London during German air attacks on the city, called "the Blitz," as well as reports from Allied planes flying missions over Europe. Murrow began to close his broadcasts with the catchphrase "good night, and good luck." The incredible eye-witness detail of Murrow's reports, along with this catchphrase, made him seem like a trusted friend, welcome in nearly every American living room. Murrow also brought together a team of younger reporters who earned nearly equal respect. The trust that Americans had for Ed Murrow extended to the rest of the news media industry.

Edward R. Murrow was a leading radio journalist of the World War II era. He helped establish new professional and ethical standards for American news media.

However, Murrow noted a decline in the quality and professionalism of American news media. On October 15, 1958, in a speech to the Radio and Television News Directors Association in Chicago, Murrow had harsh words for the new medium of TV, with its emphasis on entertainment and advertising, instead of factual and unbiased reporting. He said that TV "insulates us from the realities of the world in which we live." Murrow probably would not have been too surprised by our new media—like Snapchat, Instagram, Twitter, Facebook, Reddit, blogs, and twenty-four-hour TV news—or the "bias crisis" that they have allowed to spread.

Weinstein's history of abusing and harassing women. This helped spark the #MeToo movement that identified scores of others like him.

Money and Media: The Beginnings of Bias

American journalists have not always been as responsible as John Peter Zenger, Megan Twohey, or Ed Murrow. In the late nineteenth and early twentieth centuries, for example, being a journalist was something like being an adventurer. Advances in printing technology made it cheaper to print papers. At the same time, Americans were spreading across the country and settling new towns and also taking their business abroad, especially to the Caribbean and South America. New towns and business centers abroad created increased demands for news. The newspaper business boomed.

Biased and sensational reporting of the explosion of the ship USS *Maine* helped spark the Spanish-American War in 1898.

While many American journalists did important work then, this demand also created openings for writers looking to make money quickly, often by publishing articles that were more fiction than fact. Editors fed the public's appetite for news, but they also fed the public's appetite for stories that confirmed their existing beliefs. Powerful publishers, too, often interfered with the papers they owned, telling the editors what to cover, and how. Sometimes, these men even "made" their news. The biases of publishing giants and individual adventurer-reporters became the biases of the American people. And in some cases, the biases of the media and the public overlapped and amplified each other, selling record numbers of papers.

"New Media," New Money, and Bias in the News Today

From the 1940s until the late 1980s, the "Big Three" television networks—ABC, CBS, and NBC—dominated the American news media landscape. Together and at any given time they might have accounted for 80 percent of TV viewership. They competed with each other for ratings and viewers, but it was a controlled competition with a limited number of players, unlike the newspaper wars of the late 1800s and early 1900s. During that time period, dozens of papers fought to scoop each other, being the first to break sensational (and often slanted) news. The three mega-networks of the mid-twentieth century struck a balance. All three enjoyed their shared spot on top. Because of this, the competition was not very radical or disruptive. They all benefitted from the status quo, or the way things were. In this period of stability Americans developed a deep trust for media figures—like Ed Murrow, Dan Rather, and Murrow's rival Walter Cronkite (who earned the nickname "The Most Trusted Man in America" for his reporting).

Newspapers worked in a similar way but on a local, rather than a national, scale. Then local papers began to merge, buy each other up, or simply close. By the middle of the twentieth century, large and medium-sized cities might have two or three old and well-established papers locked in a stable competition for readers.

This stability allowed for the professionalization of the news media industry. That means that reporters and editors at news stations and papers who took their jobs seriously helped to raise standards and to make reporting fair and fact-based. Many believed a journalist's chief value to be integrity, or an unbending honesty.

However, in the 1990s, the news media landscape started to change again. As happened one hundred years earlier, this change was driven by new media technologies, new media consumer appetites, and new sources of money.

Cable TV and the Twenty-Four-Hour News Cycle

The Big Three were broadcast networks. This means their content traveled through radio waves sent, or "broadcast," to individual viewers' TV antennas. People in distant,

In 1986, CNN broadcast live footage of the space shuttle
Challenger breaking up mid-flight.

often rural communities, however, could not always
receive broadcast signals sent from TV towers in the big
cities. Over time, innovators developed a way of taking
these signals and transmitting them farther, through
cables. This technological change, though, had a much
greater effect than simply bringing ABC, NBC, and CBS
programming to small towns. Now, media entrepreneurs
had a chance to bypass the major networks and provide
content on new channels. More channels meant more

competition. And when new players enter any competition, they tend to change the way the game is played.

Suddenly, beginning in the 1990s, there were children's channels and channels for the whole family. There were channels for history, sports, cooking, crafts, construction, science, cartoons, and religious groups. There were more sitcoms than ever before. Entertainment programming began seriously competing with news for viewers' attention. Satellites only sped this up.

At the same time, satellite and cable technology had allowed two new bigger competitors to enter the news game with the Big Three: Fox and CNN. It might once have excited viewers and captured attention to broadcast Dan Rather reporting from the middle of a hurricane. But in 1986, CNN broadcast live footage of the space shuttle *Challenger* breaking up during liftoff, killing all seven astronauts onboard. Now, TV news reports were taking even greater risks, while videographers and producers were adapting filming techniques from Hollywood. While reporters had delivered the news from active war zones in Germany, Korea, and Vietnam, none of these broadcasts were quite as visually or narratively gripping as CNN reporters Peter Arnett and Bernard Shaw interviewing Iraqi officials inside Baghdad in 1991. They were reporting minute by minute as the Gulf War unfolded, which was the US response to the Iraqi invasion of Kuwait. Ten years later, Fox, shot to the top after September 11, 2001. That's when nineteen terrorists linked to the Islamist group al-Qaeda hijacked airplanes and redirected them toward four targets, including the World Trade Center, or "Twin Towers," in New York City. This time, Fox offered not only live coverage, but also passionate commentary from pundits—a form of news that mixed in opinion.

While the look and feel of news began to change, the most reliable way to beat competitors was still to scoop them. This put pressure on both TV networks and news channels to seek out stories more aggressively and publish them earlier. That competition gave rise to what we call the twenty-four-hour news cycle, a constant, round-the-clock broadcasting and publication of news. In the middle of the twentieth century, Americans read a morning and an evening paper and watched the evening news. By the end of the century, an American couldn't go to the supermarket, airport, shopping mall, or dentist's office—at any time of day—without encountering some TV that was showing breaking news.

This increased competition and constant innovation in the way that news was delivered meant increased pressure to evolve with viewers' tastes and interests. Media owners, producers, and editors realized that Americans might respect integrity, but integrity doesn't always capture attention. What did capture attention was sensational and shocking visual reporting on wars, disasters, and tragedies; a new and intense focus on the relationships and behavior of celebrities; and provocative opinions. The ratings didn't lie. The American people wanted these things. So the news industry reshaped itself to deliver them.

The Internet and New Media

Just as the cable revolution was remaking TV (and print) news, another, even bigger change was brewing: the internet. By the 1990s many American homes had computers hooked up to this information superhighway. Naturally, some early pioneers used this new tool to relay news. One such individual was Matt Drudge, a Hollywood resident with no background in journalism. In the mid-1990s he began a weekly email to friends and friends-of-friends, containing political and entertainment-industry news, tips, gossip, and commentary. It eventually evolved from an email to a website.

Called the Drudge Report, this venture in new media (meaning a new method of conveying content, other than the traditional movies, radio, TV, and print) shot to prominence in 1998 when it became the first outlet to report on a major White House scandal. Essentially, a computer hobbyist with no professional or academic training in journalism had beaten the Big Three. Not only that, but he had also beaten all of their cable and satellite competitors and all of the newspapers and magazines in the nation by scooping a major story.

Cable TV had introduced a few hundred competitors to challenge the Big Three and, to a lesser extent, newspapers and magazines. The internet would be even more revolutionary, introducing hundreds of thousands of new websites, blogs, video providers, and Twitter accounts. All of these sources would come to compete for attention with established media businesses. The people behind these new media sources would, for the most part, be more or less like Matt Drudge. They lacked academic or professional backgrounds in journalism and lacked a commitment to the journalistic professional's traditional standards or values. Yet they did have a talent for getting attention on the World Wide Web.

Targeted Advertising Warps the Web

Internet news sources aren't just competing for attention. They are also competing for money from advertisements. Advertisers found massive new markets online. They also found promoting their businesses online to be cheaper and more effective than paying for TV spots or whole-page ads in major newspapers. They could reach more people, for less. As advertisers began pulling their money from TV and print, these traditional news sources felt even more pressure to adapt to the new styles and methods of online news.

One thing online content providers and advertisers alike learned early is the internet's potential for building—and then advertising to—small, customized audiences. Some news and opinion websites began to cater mostly to liberal audiences. Others began to cater mostly to conservatives. As businesses learned to study their customer bases, they often found that certain products did better with potential customers from different backgrounds, or with different ages, religious beliefs, or political leanings. Placing an ad in a newspaper or on a television program reaches people from different backgrounds and with

ANOTHER NEW MEDIA MODEL: AXIOS

Not all of the innovators who would bring news to the internet were newcomers to journalism and media. Some of the people behind the biggest changes in the way we find, consume, and share news media were veteran journalists who left traditional TV and print careers for the internet.

Jim VandeHei was a White House correspondent for the *Washington Post*, a 141-year-old newspaper. In 2007, he decided to leave and co-found Politico, a news organization based on the web, though it also produced a paper and a magazine. Using the tools of the web, Politico established new practices that the rest of the news industry would soon adopt. These included hiring writers who could also shoot video and take pictures and using morning and midday email briefings to build a loyal (some would say *addicted*) audience.

But after a decade at Politico, VandeHei saw change coming even bigger than the internet. He saw that smartphones would do to the desktop computer what the desktop computer had done to print and TV.

Following the 2016 presidential election, VandeHei and Politico White House correspondent Mike Allen left that organization to co-found Axios. Their mission statement declared "Media is broken—and too often a scam." The internet, they believed, had made news media biased, shallow, sloppy, and often deceptive. The Axios model would have no banner ads, no misleading clickbait headlines, and no content that wasn't "worthy" of a reader's time. There was one massive break from the old newspaper model of reporting. On Axios, stories would almost always be under three hundred words—sometimes with bullet points—for easy reading on phone screens.

It remains to be seen if this new model promises more or less bias in future news. The site's commitment to delivering information quickly suggests there's less of a chance for bias to slip in. But at the same time, Axios has the habit of immediately reporting what is essentially insider political gossip. Skipping over in-depth research and the practice of consulting with multiple sources means that the site may end up reflecting the biases of whomever talked to the Axios reporters last. Meanwhile, the site is funded by massive corporate sponsors like Boeing, J. P. Morgan, and British Petroleum. Instead of running traditional ads, these companies sponsor content—writing and video that look just like Axios posts.

Is it better to have bias in plain sight like this? Only savvy and critical readers can decide.

different beliefs. More than half of those people might not be interested. To be as attractive to advertisers as websites with narrower audiences, some traditional news outlets like newspapers and TV networks began abandoning their old standards of unbiased reporting. Instead they began presenting more opinion and entertainment and less rigorously "fair" and fact-based news.

Bias Unbound

The rise of cable TV gave today's audiences an appetite for round-the-clock news, which puts pressure on reporters to produce more stories. Increased costs of producing news have led to the collapse of major, longstanding publications and other news outlets. In turn, experienced journalists lost their jobs. Into that vacuum rushed new, profit-craving publications and inexperienced journalists. The internet lowers barriers for making news, allowing thousands of bloggers and small teams of writers to compete for audiences—and advertising dollars. Websites are in direct competition with newspapers, magazines, and TV and radio stations. As a result, more of these traditional outlets continue to collapse. The ones that remain churn out stories at faster and faster rates. Journalists spend less time researching and reporting to meet demand for content. Internet advertising starts to target individuals based on their identity, location, and buying history. Advertisers continue to leave traditional media, and more news outlets close. New media publications start to cater to more specific audiences—

primarily Democrats or primarily Republicans, or to even smaller affinity and identity groups. This makes their sites more attractive to advertisers. One huge cost of this practice is a fracturing of the American news-consuming public. Instead of getting more or less the same stories from a handful of sources, Americans now get very different takes on the news. Sometimes news readers get different news altogether.

In this atmosphere, and with these economic pressures on media outlets, new and old, bias is not ignored. It's not even tolerated. Bias is *encouraged.*

Media literacy means recognizing bias in the media sources you use *and* in the media sources the people around you use.

How to Win the Fight Against Bias

I n the internet age, there are more potential sources for getting news and information than at any other time in human history. Books, magazines, papers, radio, TV, and websites, as well as online newsletters, podcasts, Snapchat, Twitter, sponsored Instagram posts, and Facebook's trending stories section all provide news. The people who decide what news makes its way to your eyes and ears don't have the same consistent commitment to controlling bias that journalists once had (or at least tried to have). Fighting bias isn't their responsibility. It's yours.

The fight against bias isn't easy, and it will never end. Luckily, though, the steps for fighting bias are easy to understand and follow:

- *Recognize* bias in the media.
- *Contextualize* information and opinions.
- *Neutralize* bias with a little simple math: add what's missing and subtract what shouldn't be there.

Recognizing Bias

To get better at recognizing and correcting bias, it will help to understand how different types of bias work. The following are just a few of the most common types.

Anchoring Bias

An anchor is designed to hold on to the first thing it catches. The human mind can be this way with information. Often, we make judgments based on the first piece of information we receive, ignoring or dismissing new information. This is called "anchoring bias."

If something important happens in the world, many people tend to draw conclusions about it based on the first news reports they read. So do the people around them. However, the first news reports on events often lack information and contain guesses and hasty judgments. Skilled media consumers will avoid making up their minds about events based on first reports and wait until more information provides a fuller picture.

Attribution Bias

To "attribute" means to assume a reason for something. For example, if you see a friend with wet hair, you might *attribute* that to recently swimming, showering, or walking in the rain. But we don't know what actually caused the wet hair. Attribution bias, then, happens when we are unfair or unreasonable in assuming the reasons for things.

If a media figure gives a reason for anything at all, test it. Does the reason seem logical? Is there a connection between the effect or event and the cause the person gave? Is there evidence to support the reason? If the answer to these questions is "no," the reporter is likely demonstrating attribution bias.

Confirmation Bias

Everybody wants to be right. Because of this, we often look for information that proves us right or confirms what we already believe to be true. This also means that we can ignore or forget information that challenges our beliefs, or recall events in ways that support our ideas, blocking memories that would complicate things.

Television news talk shows encourage attribution bias because it's entertaining to watch other people propose and then argue about the reasons for current events.

No matter how trustworthy a source appears, check on how that source has covered the subject previously. Has the writer been overly critical of the subject? Has the writer been overly kind and forgiving? It's possible that this writer suffers from a confirmation bias. If the writer has already made up her mind about the subject's character, she is likely to seek out information that confirms her beliefs and ignore information that challenges them.

Halos and Horns

Two specific types of confirmation bias are the "halo effect" and the "horn effect." These get their names from saints' halos and devils' horns. Basically, both refer to the habit of taking one positive or negative trait in a person or thing and using this to make positive or negative judgments about the person's other traits. Brands and companies can have halos and horns too. For example, many people associate Subway with healthy food and McDonald's with unhealthy food. In one study, scientists showed people pictures of Subway and McDonald's meals with exactly the same calorie count. Overwhelmingly, the subjects assumed that the Subway meal had significantly fewer calories. Here, the halo and horn effects are working at the same time.

When reading, watching, or listening to news about people—from politicians to celebrities and small-time criminals—think about the way that those people appear to the audience and to the media. Is it a celebrity with a history of crude and obnoxious behavior? Is it a politician known for fairness, kindness, and charity work? Be prepared for the facts from later reports to contradict early reports from media figures who let themselves be tricked by "halos" and "horns."

Framing Bias

Different frames can change the way a picture looks without changing the picture itself. We can frame information too. Journalists often report the same facts but frame them differently. This leads audiences to come to different conclusions about the same information.

Imagine that two TV news stations report the same facts about a deadly attack. They report the same time, location, and number of people injured or killed. But one station calls it a "tragedy," and another calls it an "act of terror." Both phrases, "tragedy," and "act of terror," carry very different meanings. They trigger very different thoughts and feelings in the audience. The two stations have framed the issue in different ways—possibly revealing biases. Try to consult several different media sources reporting on the same subject. Look for the different frames they use.

Prejudice and Favoritism

One of the simplest types of bias is prejudice. To be prejudiced is to have positive or negative feelings toward a person based only on that person's membership in a group. Prejudice can be rooted in race, religion, class, educational background, nationality, age, sex, sexual orientation, or affiliation with a team. It can be based on any group identity. More often than not, we tend to make more positive judgments about people who share our identity groups.

To fight prejudice, try to identify groups that connect or distance a reporter and her subject. Are they the same race? Did they attend the same school? Are they members of the same political party or movement? All of these might be sources of positive or negative prejudice.

In general, get information from many sources. Ideally, these sources will be consistently high-quality while coming from many different identity groups.

Contextualizing Content in Your Media Environment

Recognizing the types of bias and understanding how they work doesn't necessarily mean that one will be able to recognize them as they appear. For a smart reader to apply what she knows about bias, contextualization is key. To contextualize means to think about things in relation to their sources and in relation to the circumstances and facts that surround them.

Zoom Out: Consider the Source

To contextualize any news media, start by identifying where the news came from. One can think of this as "zooming out." Switch focus from the individual story to the big picture, or the source that produced the story.

If a source is familiar, consider whether that source (an individual reporter or a company or website) has a history of biased reporting or if there is any reason to suspect that this particular piece of news might be biased. If a source is unfamiliar or unknown, research it. Google it. Ask friends, parents, and teachers about it. Look for opinions from both people who like and who dislike the source.

Then take the time to examine other content—articles, analysis, videos, or podcasts—from the same source. Do any of these demonstrate a more obvious bias? For example, perhaps the first article from a website or print source seems believable. But another from the same site lacks evidence, mixes reporting and opinion, or includes unreasonable statements. Go back and take a closer look at the first article. There are different giveaways for new media sources. A smart listener might pick up clues in the tone of voice that a podcast host uses when talking about certain subjects. There might be patterns of bias in the types of images that appear in video reporting.

Remember, too, that even well-known and respected news sources are biased. This is simply because newsmakers are human. Taken together, all of the reporters and editors at any institution will, statistically, lean one way or another on any given issue. Does all of the content together tell a biased story? Even if it does, this doesn't mean the reporters are unprofessional or have low standards. The keen consumer just has to take news from that source with a critical eye and ear.

MACHINE BIAS

Most of the time when experts talk about bias, they mean *human* bias. But as computer technology gets more advanced, studies have repeatedly shown that machines can be biased too.

Machines can't go with their gut, like humans. Instead, they use mathematical equations to make decisions. For example, some smartphones and computers can be unlocked by looking into the camera. In this case, the computer tries to identify different features of a face. These features include eye color, the angle of cheekbones, and nose length. The computer tries to match these features against those in pictures that the computer has taken and stored. If enough features match, the computer "decides" to unlock itself.

Machines don't have any feelings. They won't feel threatened if new information challenges the data they already have stored. Yet bias still creeps in. The trouble is with the equations that computers use to make decisions—and the humans who write the equations.

For example, many states in America have adopted risk assessment computer programs in the criminal justice system. Scientists originally designed these programs to study what factors might make a criminal released from prison more likely to lead a productive life or commit another crime. They take in information about an individual, such as educational background, criminal history, and the answers to questions that may reveal something about a person's values or decision-making process. Then they assign a score on a scale, sort of like a grade. In recent years, states have begun

Humans can build bias into the machines they create. Artificial intelligence applications, like facial recognition software, have exhibited bias.

introducing these programs into the courts. Now, they help judges to make very important decisions. These programs might influence whether or not a judge accepts a defendant's plea bargain (an admission of guilt in exchange for less time behind bars), how high to set bail, and even how long a convicted criminal's prison sentence should be.

The nonprofit journalism organization ProPublica investigated these programs and found that they were overwhelmingly biased. The programs consistently gave black subjects higher risk assessments than white subjects. They also proved frighteningly inaccurate. They often gave low risk assessments to convicts who went on to commit future crimes. They also often gave higher risk assessments to individuals who would have no further run-ins with the law.

Compare and Contrast: Reading "Around" the News

Once you know something about a news item's source, the next step is to zoom even farther out. Take the first source's ongoing coverage of a subject (in multiple stories, videos, or other types of content produced over a period of time) and compare it to coverage from other sources that might do the job differently. For example, to test for bias in coverage about a planned wind energy farm in Wisconsin, read several stories from local Wisconsin papers. Are there differences in the coverage at this level? What about differences in coverage from national or international sources—like the *Guardian* and the *Wall Street Journal*? What about differences in coverage from nontraditional new media sources? Understanding the way other sources and content producers cover a topic will make it much easier to spot evidence of bias in the first source.

Critical Questions

After considering a source, and comparing that source's coverage of a subject with coverage from other sources, zoom back in. Don't forget everything known about the source, of course. Keep all of that in mind, but focus instead on the original news piece. Start to ask critical questions aimed at identifying bias. Begin with questions like "Who is writing?", "Who is paying?", and "Who benefits?" Then add more questions as needed.

Neutralizing Bias and Sharing Your Analysis

Once you have contextualized a news item, the bias will be "neutralized." Luckily, the brain is good at doing this kind of work. If a reader or viewer has asked the right questions and gathered all the information necessary to put a news item in context, it will be surprisingly easy to recognize bias. The brain will raise red flags at suspicious images, clips, headlines, quotes, and other content.

The real challenge will be expressing this automatic analysis to others. This is especially hard when talking to others who might not have trained themselves to think about bias or read this closely.

Recognizing and correcting bias requires close attention to language, word by word.

Everyone consumes information, which means there is no escaping bias. But actively seeking out bias provides a chance to learn more about the world than consuming information from the least biased media sources and ignoring all the rest.

Putting Your Skills into Action

You can only tackle bias one story at a time, so start with the story in front of you. For example, let's say there's a newspaper story about the governor's plan to build a bridge. No matter the subject or the source, you need to ask the same critical questions of any piece of news you encounter. You can imagine asking these questions of our example news story. Then, try the same questions on a real story, wherever you get your news.

What Are You Hearing?

Oftentimes, bias rises to the surface of a piece of writing. It might even be obvious in the headline. "Governor Unveils Bridge Plans, Residents Protest," is a neutral headline. It gives voice to both sides of this debate and

The techniques for recognizing bias are the same no matter where you get your news.

avoids language that characterizes either one. "Bridge Progress Hits Roadblock: Residents Raise Outcry," however, uses colorful language ("roadblock" and "raise outcry") and opinion ("progress") to characterize the governor as right and the opponents of the bridge wrong. The same telltale language—often colorful verbs, or nouns and adjectives that present opinion—will appear throughout the body of a story.

What Are You Seeing?

Pictures (and videos) convey bias too. This article might run with a picture of a road clogged with traffic. It might run alongside a picture of wildlife on an undeveloped piece of land. Each picture expresses only one point of view. The first suggests the bridge is necessary to calm traffic. The second suggests it will disrupt wildlife and destroy habitats.

Who Is Writing?

Open up an internet browser and search the writer's name. You can start within the news company's site. Then go further with Google or another search engine. Has the author written many articles about the governor? Has the writer tweeted about the bridge? Can you find hard evidence of bias elsewhere that would affect how you read this story? (Of course, it's always best to ask an adult before searching social media.)

Who Is Paying?

Find the owner of the news organization that produced this article, and then search to see if they have political affiliations, or a history of treating political parties, politicians, industries, businesses, or causes a certain way. You might even head to the Federal Election Commission's website and search that owner's political donations (https://classic.fec.gov/finance/disclosure/norindsea.shtml). Has the owner donated to the governor? Has the owner been critical of large public spending projects like this bridge plan? Especially at newspapers and longer-established media outlets, an owner's political, religious, or ideological beliefs are not necessarily going to influence individual writers and editors. However, if you've noticed other signs of bias, the owner's history is an important factor to consider.

Who Is Missing?

Identify the stakeholders, or people and groups that are most affected by the issues at the heart of the story. People who have to drive to get to work may be in favor of the bridge. People who live close to the site of the proposed bridge construction may be against it. Has the writer talked to all of the stakeholders? If not, what are the silences saying?

Who Benefits?

You've probably already identified who will benefit from the bridge in this scenario. But who benefits from the story being told right now? Does calling attention to the story help the governor push through the bridge plans? Does it give energy to the resistance? If one person or group obviously benefits from a story—and its timing—that person or group might sit very close to the reporter's ear.

Who Is the Intended Audience?

If a media source targets a certain audience, its news content will almost always reflect that audience's bias. Conservative talk radio coverage of this bridge will reflect the conservative take on the bridge. It will either be in favor of its effect on business or against the excessive government spending, for example. Local alternative papers (which generally play more to activist audiences or groups left or right of the center) may focus on supposed government corruption or the disruption the bridge could cause. For example, the bridge might have a negative effect on local homeowners or animal populations. A mainstream daily newspaper will likely aim for the middle of the road. Moderation,

Journalists at local alternative papers often write from a different perspective than journalists at mainstream publications.

too, can be a kind of bias, willfully ignoring facts to avoid controversy.

Remember that the answer to any one of these critical questions will not give you definite proof of bias. And even if you do sense bias, that might not mean you should discredit the story, the writer, or the publication as totally untrustworthy. However, if you get in the habit of asking *all* of the questions above whenever you consume the news (and no matter the source), your mind will start to filter out automatically the writer's opinions. You'll be left with a road map of only facts, and new, specific questions to ask to get the rest of the picture.

Going Public: How to Help Friends, Family, and Others Recognize Bias

Recognizing bias is the easy part. Everyone lives, works, plays, creates, and consumes media in a community. People have an obligation to share what they know with the rest of that community and to call out and correct bias whenever it enters that community's conversation. This isn't easy. However, if you keep a few key points in your own mind, you may be surprised by your ability to change others' minds.

Don't Let Debates Go Very Far Without the Facts

Conversations about the news can be heated. One person challenges a news story. Another defends it. A third jumps in with a different take. But often, no one has hard numbers, facts, or trustworthy sources to back anything

BARBARA HAMEL AND DAVID MIKKELSON

Barbara Hamel met David Mikkelson online in a forum for people who liked weird folklore. Both were fussy about facts and persistent about finding proof. They eventually married and started a website, Snopes, dedicated to fact-checking modern-day myths that touched on everything from marshmallows to magic. After September 11, 2001, however, Hamel turned to the website and her fact-checking efforts there as a way to process her grief and shock. She started by tackling a rumor that the sixteenth century astrologer, chemist, and poet Nostradamus had predicted the attacks. Traffic on the site shot up, and soon other rumors, conspiracy theories, and biased reports were flooding in. Mikkelson and Hamel started fact-checking as many as they could. Their website took on a new significance. Rather than indulging a hobby, they were offering a service that thousands and eventually millions of Americans would rely on for a dose of certainty in uncertain times.

As traffic grew, so did the website's revenue. Mikkelson managed the technical aspects of the website while Hamel

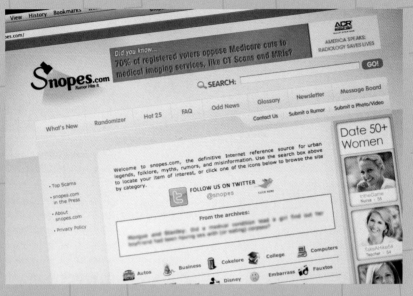

Many Americans trust Snopes, the fact-checking website,
to watch and correct the mainstream news media.
Barbara Hamel and David Mikkelson created the site.

did the bookkeeping. Both selected topics, researched, wrote, and fact-checked each other's posts. While Hamel eventually split from Mikkelson and stepped away from her role in the site, her more than fifteen years there helped to shape news media in the twenty-first century. Snopes is proof that the internet doesn't only hurt traditional media—it can also hold it to a higher standard.

Recognizing bias isn't enough. We also need to be able to talk about bias with other members of our families and communities.

up. Luckily, you have the internet at your fingertips—and the critical mind and media literacy training necessary to use it well. If you walk into the middle of an argument about the news—or if you call out media bias and someone else dismisses you—pull out your phone or turn to a computer and let the facts speak for themselves, before the discussion gets too emotional.

Be careful, though. Resist the temptation simply to Google points of view that clash with the one you're trying to disprove. If you do this, you're likely to find only more biased sources. Instead, learn to use data sets, like the FEC record of all individual political contributions, scientific and academic organizations' data, or databases that you may be able to access through your school. You should also explore reputable sites dedicated to fact-checking. These include Snopes, PolitiFact, OpenSources, Media Bias / Fact Check, and FactCheck. These are subject to error too. Sometimes biased people quickly shout "bias" back at these sites when they feel attacked. The nice thing about sites like Snopes and PolitiFact, though, is that they show their work. They explain how they came to their conclusions, so you can follow the trail of evidence.

Fact-checking websites like PolitiFact are excellent resources for identifying bias.

Acknowledge and Correct Your Own Biases

Constantly test your opinions and beliefs. Be open to others testing them too. Examine your own conclusions the way you would examine an article online or in a magazine. If you change your mind, even about a deeply held belief, that's something to celebrate. Showing your ability to change your mind when the facts demand it also demonstrates to others in your community that you're a reasonable, thoughtful, humble, and trustworthy person.

Be Respectful

Remember that finding evidence of bias in another person's point of view doesn't make him or her bad or stupid. Recognizing bias isn't a chance for you to beat

CHANGE MY VIEW

Head to the comments sections on Facebook, YouTube, Instagram, Reddit, and any of the news media sites that feature them, and you will find users demonstrating their weaknesses for the halo and horn effects, attribution bias, framing bias, prejudice, and more. You might even get the impression that people turn to the internet to express their biases *knowingly*, on purpose, and without real consequences.

But that isn't true everywhere online. Kal Turnbull, a Scottish musician, was seventeen years old when he realized that he and his friends all essentially thought the same way, holding similar opinions (and, probably, biases). He turned to Reddit, the social news and discussion website, to form an online community of people who want to have their views carefully, respectfully, and vigorously challenged. That community is called "Change My View." Today, users post views ranging from "The government should do your taxes for you" to "Humanity's ultimate goal should be to become a spacefaring civilization."

Users then wait for others to challenge them. Commenters jump in and—almost always respectfully— present new information, point out illogical reasoning, and check bias. Carefully chosen moderators police name-calling, rudeness, and unnecessary aggression as well as off-topic or excessive jokes and simple agreement that doesn't carry the conversation forward. When posters have their views changed, they award deltas (the mathematical symbol for change) to the user whose comment flipped them.

someone. If you can have a respectful, reasonable, and calm discussion about what you think might be someone else's bias, both of you will have an opportunity to test your beliefs, your instincts, and your news media literacy skills—together.

Good Gardening: Caring for Your Media Environment

Remember that in today's media environment, no one is a passive consumer of news. Everyone actively participates in the flow of information and ideas—often by writing or capturing video and photos, but also by "liking," sharing, commenting, and discussing with friends, family, and strangers in person.

Therefore, everyone has a responsibility to themselves and to others when creating or consuming news media. Think of fighting news media bias like caring for a small but shared garden. No one has to care for the whole forest. Like Barbara Hamel and Kal Turnbull, focus on a small corner of the media landscape. Weed out the bad (biased, false, or poor-quality content), and support the good (fair, evidence-based, and high-quality content). Do this and your garden will grow stronger. It will nourish you and the people around you. Your efforts may even inspire others to do the same.

GLOSSARY

anchoring bias A type of bias that describes the human tendency to rely too much on the first piece of evidence that one receives when making a decision.

attribution The act of giving a reason or believing in a reason for something. "Attribution bias" describes any reasoning errors one makes when trying to identify reasons for one's own behavior or the behavior of others.

bias An unfair or unreasonable inclination in favor of or against one thing, person, or group compared with another.

broadcast networks Television stations transmitted through radio waves received by an individual viewer's television antenna or satellite. (ABC, CBS, and NBC are broadcast networks.)

clickbait Internet content where the main purpose is to attract attention and encourage visitors to click on a link to a particular web page.

consume Take in.

contextualize To think about or explain something in its context. That is, taking into account its origin and background and related information rather than considering it as an isolated idea, object, or event.

framing bias The human tendency to react to the same information in different ways depending on how it is presented.

ideology A set of beliefs or values, usually based on a certain system of political ideas.

libel A published false statement that is damaging to a person's reputation.

media The main sources of mass communication: newspapers, magazines, radio stations, TV channels, movies, content-producing websites, and online social platforms.

news feed A section of an online social platform that contains a collection of suggested and sponsored content of a personal, informational, or entertainment-focused nature.

passive The opposite of active.

prejudice A negative feeling toward an individual based on that individual's identity as a member of a certain group.

process Make sense of.

pundit An expert in a subject or field who is frequently called on to give opinions about it to the general public, often through some form of mass or mainstream media.

status quo A Latin phrase meaning "the way things are."

verify Confirm as true.

FURTHER INFORMATION

Books

Harris, Duchess, and Laura K. Murray. *Uncovering Bias in the News*. North Mankato, MN: ABDO Publishing, 2017.

Vance, Lucian. *Fake News and Media Bias*. New York: Greenhaven Publishing, 2018.

Websites

Best News Sources for Kids
https://www.commonsensemedia.org/lists/best-news-sources-for-kids

Search by your age to find respected, balanced news sources.

News Literacy
http://www.gamesforchange.org/studentchallenge/la/news-literacy/#1508500623475-e64fe171-14a5

Explore resources, videos, and activities to hone your news literacy skills.

Videos

How to Choose Your News – Damon Brown

https://www.youtube.com/watch?v=q-Y-z6HmRgI

In this TED Ed video, Damon Brown explains how news has changed over time and why it's important to get news straight from the source.

Media Literacy

https://www.youtube.com/watch?v=oQMSKRrDjB4

BrainPOP presents an engaging animated video about choosing news sources wisely.

News Literacy

https://www.youtube.com/watch?v=GOI_13LFQVw

Time for Kids interviews students and teachers to provide a crash course in critical engagement with the news.

BIBLIOGRAPHY

Angwin, Julia, Jeff Larson, Surya Mattu, and Lauren Kirchner. "Machine Bias." ProPublica, May 23, 2016. https://www.propublica.org/article/machine-bias-risk-assessments-in-criminal-sentencing.

Briscoe Center for American History. "Dan Rather: American Journalist." Retrieved March 13, 2018. https://danratherjournalist.org/ground/natural-disasters#Opal.

Dana, Rebecca. "Lovely Canoe-gate Girl Tells All!" *Observer*, October 24, 2005. http://observer.com/2005/10/lovely-canoegate-girl-tells-all.

Dean, Michelle. "Snopes and the Search for Facts in a Post-Fact World." *Wired*, September 20, 2017. https://www.wired.com/story/snopes-and-the-search-for-facts-in-a-post-fact-world.

Encyclopedia Britannica. "John Peter Zenger." Retrieved March 13, 2018. https://www.britannica.com/biography/John-Peter-Zenger.

Goodwin, Doris Kearns. *The Bully Pulpit: Theodore Roosevelt and the Golden Age of Journalism*. New York: Simon and Schuster, 2013.

Hansen Liane, and David Folkenflick. "The Power of the 24-Hour News Cycle." NPR, May 29, 2005. https://www.npr.org/templates/story/story.php?storyId=4671485.

Heffernan, Virginia. "Our Best Hope for Civil Discourse Online Is on ... Reddit." *Wired*, January 16, 2018. https://www.wired.com/story/free-speech-issue-reddit-change-my-view.

Kovach, Bill, and Tom Rosenstiel. *Warp Speed: America in the Age of Mixed Media*. New York: The Century Foundation, 1999.

Otero, Vanessa. "The Chart, Version 1.0: Original Reasoning and Methodology." All Generalizations Are False, December 19, 2016. http://www.allgeneralizationsarefalse.com/the-reasoning-and-methodology-behind-the-chart.

Persico, Joseph E. *Edward R. Murrow: An American Original*. New York: McGraw Hill, 1988.

Vinton, Kate. "These 15 Billionaires Own America's News Media Companies." *Forbes*, June 1, 2016. https://www.forbes.com/sites/katevinton/2016/06/01/these-15-billionaires-own-americas-news-media-companies/#6c531c56660a.

INDEX

ABOUT THE AUTHOR

Aidan M. Ryan is a writer, publisher, and educator. He has published essays in *Traffic East*, *Buffalo News*, and CNN.com; music criticism in the *Skinny*; and interviews in *Rain Taxi* and the *White Review*. Ryan is an adjunct professor of English at Canisius College and a teaching artist at the Just Buffalo Writing Center. He is also a founding partner and managing editor of Foundlings Press, an independent literary publishing house based in Buffalo, New York.